Do Cats Really
Have Nine Lives?

Illustrations by
John Rice, Tom Powers, and Mimi Powers
Cover illustration by Tom Powers

Text copyright © 1993 by Highlights for Children
Illustrations copyright © 1993 by Boyds Mills Press
Published by Bell Books
Boyds Mills Press, Inc.
A Highlights Company
910 Church Street
Honesdale, Pennsylvania 18431

Cataloging-in-Publication Data
Myers, Jack, 7/10/13
    Do cats really have nine lives?
and other questions about your world / answered by
Highlights Science Editor Jack Myers, Ph.D.
[64] p. : col. ill. ; cm.
Summary: Answers to children's questions about the world.
Many questions taken from columns in Highlights for Children.
ISBN 1-56397-089-9 HC; ISBN 1-56397-215-8 pb
1. —Juvenile Literature. [1. Science.]   I. Series   II. Title.
500—dc20   1993
Library of Congress Catalog Card Number: 91-77713
First edition, 1993
Book designed by Bob Feldgus and Jeffrey E. George
The text of this book is set in 11-point Century Schoolbook.
The illustrations are ink, watercolor, and colored pencil.
Distributed by St. Martin's Press
Printed in the United States of America
Reinforced trade edition
10 9 8 7 6 5 4 3 2 1

Do Cats Really Have Nine Lives?

And Other Questions about Your World

Answered by

Highlights Science Editor
Jack Myers, Ph.D.

BELL BOOKS
BOYDS MILLS PRESS

Welcome Aboard!

You have joined our club. We are the curious, wondering about all the interesting things that happen in our world. When we don't know, we ask. Here in the records of our club you will find answers to some of the questions you have wondered about.

For the past thirty years readers of Highlights for Children have been asking me questions. And I have been helping them find answers. There have been questions I could not answer and questions that I think no one could answer. Science has always been like that, and it is like that today even in the world's greatest laboratories. It is our ignorance—what we don't know—that drives us to learn more. That's what science is all about.

I have been fortunate in having as friends many scientists who have helped me find answers. To all of them we are grateful, for they have broadened our understanding.

In this book some of the answers have been written directly by someone who had a much greater understanding of the questions than I—the late Dr. Osmond P. Breland. Each of his answers will be acknowledged by his initials.

Jack Myers

Jack Myers, Ph.D.

Why does aging wood on a house turn black?

Sarah Adams
Griffin, Georgia

Since I did not have an answer to your question, I wrote to the Forest Products Laboratory in Madison, Wisconsin. The scientists there know nearly all there is to know about wood. They sent me a bulletin that contains an answer to your question.

When exposed to the weather, dark-colored woods may become lighter but light-colored woods usually become darker. In time almost any wood ends up as black or some shade of gray and its surface becomes rough. Wood is made mostly of fibers of cellulose, the same stuff that makes up cotton. Wood is hard because the cellulose fibers are cemented together by another stuff called lignin. The lignin and the colored substances in wood are slowly broken down by light and washed out by rain. That gives the wood a rough surface and tends to make it lighter in color. But while all this is going on, micro-organisms, like fungi, may grow on the wood and add their dark colors to make it gray and blotchy or sometimes even black.

You can see why we usually coat wood with a paint or stain to protect it against the weather and prevent all these changes from happening.

Will you please explain to me how the back cover of a matchbook is attracted to the tip of a match to make fire?

Kim Meredith
Newark, New Jersey

You are right that it takes both the tip of the match and a special surface to make fire.

However, the two do not attract each other. The match tip must be rubbed on the striking surface.

The idea is the same as the Indian way of making a fire by rubbing two sticks together next to some easy-to-burn stuff like fine wood shavings. We need something that gets hot by friction and something easy to burn. Chemists found things much easier to burn and invented matches that start to burn with only a little friction.

The head of a safety match usually has a chemical called potassium chlorate and some charcoal or sulfur. The striking surface has some red phosphorous and fine sand. That combination lights easily, so it does not take much rubbing to make the match tip start to burn.

Of course, anything that easy to burn ought to be handled carefully. It is easy to get fingers burned by careless use of matches.

How does fire get its colors?

Emily Glenn
Delaware, Ohio

Most things that burn contain the element carbon. It burns by combining with oxygen to make carbon dioxide. But almost always some of the carbon is not completely burned and comes off as a black smoke. While the carbon particles are in the hot flame, they give a yellow glow. So, most fires are yellow.

For some things, like burning wood, other colors besides yellow may appear in the flames. I think they come mostly from minerals in the wood. Although they do not burn, some metals give off special colors when they get hot. In fact, color in a flame is used by chemists as tests for some metals. I will make a list of a few elements with their colors in a flame:

sodium—yellow
potassium—violet
copper—green
strontium—red

I think some of these are also used to give the special colors in fireworks.

How does fire turn into ash after it burns?

Anne Tegtmeier
Arvado, Colorado

I think the fire itself, the flame, does not turn into ash. It may seem to you almost the same thing if I say that ash is left after a fire has burned. Or, we could say that fire can turn wood into ash. Actually, the ash is stuff that was there in the wood to start with, a small part of the wood that the fire could not burn.

Except for gasoline and natural gas, most of the things we burn leave some ash. Ash comes from minerals. The ash left by burning wood comes from minerals that a tree needed and took up from the soil by its roots.

3

I have a dog and a cat that seem as if they are always communicating. I want to know how this is done.

Jenny Rudd
Jeffersonville, Indiana

If you carefully watch your dog and cat, I think you will learn the answer. I think you will find that they use what we call body language. People use this all the time, even though we also have a language of words.

People frown or scowl or grin, sometimes hunch their shoulders, and make gestures with their hands. If you think about this idea and then watch your cat and dog, I think you will see that they use body language, too.

Do cats really have nine lives?

Shawna Clark
Michigan City, Indiana

I guess both of us have heard that saying many times. We don't really believe it, but there must be a reason for the saying. There is.

You and other animals have a reflex that helps you stay balanced. It is called the **righting reflex.** This works so neatly that you may not have noticed it. A time to feel it happen is when you are walking and your foot slips. Then a number of muscles in your legs, your back, maybe even your shoulders suddenly work to try to keep your body upright.

Cats are world champions in having a well-developed righting reflex. If a cat starts to fall out of a tree, it twists its whole body in midair and lands on its feet. So, cats often survive falls that would kill most animals. I think that's where the idea came from that cats may have more than one life.

What I cannot answer is where the *nine* comes from. It might mean that a cat will survive a bad fall nine out of ten times. Or maybe nine is just a nice number. Or maybe you can think of a better reason.

I have a cat. It's all black. My question is, at nighttime when it is a full moon, why do my cat's eyes light up?

Nicole Robinson
Baltimore, Maryland

The eyes of other animals are very much like yours. Light gets in through the pupil, the little dark spot in the center, and is focused by the lens to make a small picture on the retina. The retina is a filmy layer of light-sensitive nerve cells at the back of the eye. In most animal eyes the retina is supported by a dark-colored layer just behind it. The dark layer absorbs any light that gets through the retina. So, the pupil of the eye looks black because very little light ever gets back out.

Some animals are nocturnal, meaning that they are active at night. And some of the nocturnal animals have eyes with a special feature. Instead of a dark layer behind the retina, they have a shiny reflecting layer called the **tapetum**. That seems like a good way for helping an eye to see in very dim light. We suppose that reflection by the tapetum doubles the chance that a light ray will fall on a light-sensitive cell of the retina.

Now we can answer your question. An eye with a tapetum also does a special trick. Some of the light that enters the pupil goes right back out the way it came in. So if you are out in the woods at night with a flashlight, the eyes of a cat or a raccoon or an alligator seem to shine right back at you.

I have a pet cat named Misty. I have noticed that her nose is wet. My friend has a dog, and its nose is wet, too. I would like to know why dogs' and cats' noses are wet?

Erin Boswell
Louisville, Kentucky

I thought that it would be easy to find an answer to that question. It isn't. A book on a lot of hard-to-answer questions has been written—and with a title exactly the same as your question. The author couldn't find a very good answer, either.

Here's what I did find out. The skin covering a dog's nose is special. It has no hair follicles that make hairs and no sweat glands. So the nose is not wet by sweat. I couldn't find reference to any special glands producing fluid in the nose.

When a dog is panting, it breathes in, mostly through the nose, and breathes out, mostly through the mouth. However, in quiet breathing, much of the breathed-out air goes through the nose. That breathed-out air is warm and very humid, and there is likely to be condensation if the outside air is cooler. That may help to keep the nose wet. And you've noticed that dogs often lick their noses with their tongues. I think that if you could lick your nose that way, your nose might be wet, too.

I think that answering your question may be difficult just because there are several parts to the answer.

How do dogs wag their tails?

Candace Drewes
Scotch Plains, New Jersey

Some kinds of dogs have long tails and some have short tails, but they are all built very much alike. The inside of a dog's tail is made up of a string of bones, something like a string of big beads. Little muscles are attached to the bones. Most dogs can hold their tails up or down, or wag them from side to side, by using these little muscles.

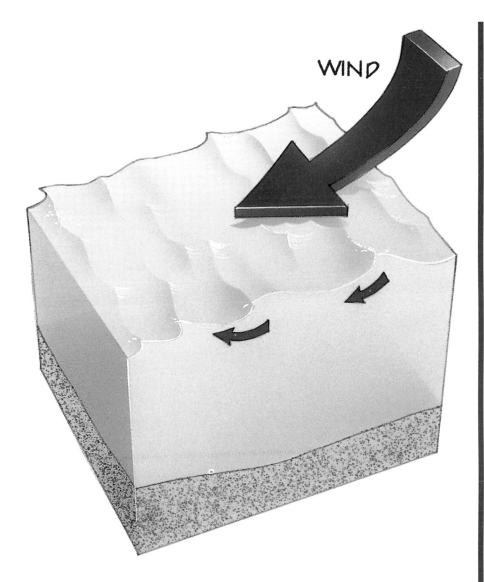

WIND

What makes waves curl as they reach the shore?

Stacey Canada
Jonesboro, Arkansas

People have been watching waves for a long time. And books have been written about them. Just as you noticed, something happens to ocean waves as they come to the shallow water near shore. Exactly how this works depends on the shape of the beach.

Let's suppose we are watching very regular ocean waves coming in toward a gradually sloping beach. As the water begins to get shallower, water movement is slowed by friction against the bottom. The waves are slowed down and pushed together. That makes each wave steeper, especially on its front side. As the water gets more shallow, the waves get steeper and steeper until they fall over and break on the front side.

Usually a wave breaks when the water depth is about $1\frac{1}{3}$ times the height of the waves. A lot more is going on inside a wave that we did not talk about. But maybe you can see why waves break as they move into shallow water.

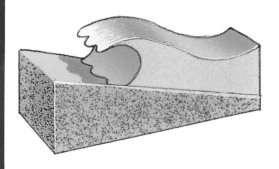

What causes waves?

Heather MacKay
Kokomo, Indiana

Most waves that you can see every day are caused by the wind. As air blows across a water surface there is a little friction between the air and water. That tends to slow down the lowest layer of air and drag along some of the upper layer of water. You have noticed that a blowing wind does not blow smoothly. Almost always it is gusty or churning around. So, the drag on the surface is uneven. That's enough to make little waves.

Once there are little waves, the wind pushes against them to make bigger waves. As the wind goes farther and farther across the ocean, the waves get bigger and farther apart.

You can make your own waves. Put a big dinner plate on the kitchen drain board and fill it almost level-full with water. Now get down close and blow across the surface of the surface of the plate. You can see why wind and waves go together.

I was wondering, if seedless grapes don't have seeds, how do they grow?

Cathy Clem
Suffolk, Virginia

I suppose you are thinking that plants grow up from seeds. And you are right. You can't get seedless grapes that way if they don't make seeds.

Many kinds of plants also can reproduce in a different way. Some part of the plant, usually a piece of the stem, is planted in the soil. It will first grow roots and then grow into a complete plant. I believe that all kinds of grapes are grown in this way.

You might like to try this idea by cutting a small section of leaves and stems from an ivy plant. Just put it in a glass of water some place in your room where it will get some light.

Be patient. Nothing will happen overnight. In time your ivy stem should begin growing roots.

What causes the seed, after the sun has shone and the rain has poured, to pop up into a plant?

Emma Chanlett-Avery
Hinton, West Virginia

A seed is already a tiny plant, an embryo all ready to grow. It also has stored food material to live on until it can put out green leaves and make its own food. And it usually has a tough outer coat to protect it until it is time to grow.

How does a seed know when it is time to grow? First, something must happen inside to get the embryo ready. Most seeds need to wait until the next spring before they start to grow. Some have to just wait, some need to get cold, some need to dry out before they are ready. After that, almost all seeds need the same things to start growing: water and warmth. So, that's why you see little plants popping up from seeds on a warm spring day after a rain.

We have an oak tree in our backyard (the reason we know that it is oak is because of its acorns). The leaves used to look like this ❦. Now they look like this ❦ and this year they started to look like this ❦! Can you explain this?

Joseph Miller
Virginia Beach, Virginia

I think you were very observant. Not many people would have noticed. And not many would have made sure it was an oak tree by its acorns.

Anyone who has spent much time looking at trees learns to recognize different kinds by the shapes of their leaves. The maple leaf is so distinctive that Canada has made it a national symbol. So we are used to the idea that each kind of tree makes its leaves in one special shape.

Now it is also true that some trees are a bit careless in making leaves. It just happens that oaks are good examples of trees that may make their leaves in patterns that are not always the same. Another example is poison ivy, which is usually a bush rather than a tree, but also does not always have exactly the same patterns for its leaves.

If you study any one kind of plant or animal, you soon discover that individuals are all alike in some ways but different in others.

It's easy to see that this is true about human beings. Wouldn't it be terrible if we were all exactly alike?

I would like to know what makes volcanoes come out of the ground. I am interested in this.

Stuart Beck
Commack, New York

Not all volcanoes are alike. Probably you are thinking about the kind that come out of the tops of mountains. Usually the whole mountain was formed by hot liquid stuff that came out of the volcano, flowed down the sides, and hardened into rock. Then we may call that whole mountain a volcano.

Sometimes volcanoes are called "windows into the earth." They tell us that way down deep the earth has a very hot and liquid core. The part of the earth where we live is the solid crust on the outside.

The hot liquid stuff of the core is called magma. It is under great pressure from the crust above. At some place where the crust is weaker, magma may be forced upward, melting rocks of the crust with its great heat. The melting rocks release gases that make the magma push upward still more.

All that bubbly hot magma tries to get out through the crust. Sometimes it quietly bubbles upward through a hole in the mountain and flows down the sides. Sometimes it is partly blocked and then builds up pressure until it violently erupts.

Volcanoes behave in different ways—some quietly, some violently. All of them are formed by the hot liquid magma that is usually deep below us in the earth.

10

I would like to know what causes an earthquake?

Stacey Sookerskoff
Saskatoon, Saskatchewan

We live on the outer crust, the wrinkled outside skin, of the earth. We think that the earth is very steady, and most of the time and in most places it is. But down underneath, slow movements are going on. If the crust were nice and flexible, it would move slowly, too—so slowly that we would not notice it.

Where the crust of the earth is very rigid and where slow movements are occurring underneath, then the crust may crack and slip a little. That makes an earthquake.

How do volcanoes affect the weather?

Christy Van Dyke
Kansas City, Kansas

The eruption of a volcano affects our weather mostly by the big cloud of dust that it sends high up into the air. At first the dust cloud may darken the earth for miles around the volcano. Then the cloud gradually gets thinner as it is mixed up by winds.

A very large cloud of dust came from the eruption of the volcano El Chichon in southern Mexico in April 1982. This was big enough to be seen in photos taken by our satellites. The cloud rose to a height of about 15 miles. There, a wind stream carried it in a narrow path all the way around the earth. Parts of the cloud could still be seen in photos three weeks later.

So far I have not seen any report about special effects of that dust cloud on our weather. Some effects are certain to have happened somewhere, just because a dust cloud reflects sunlight and will cause at least a small local, cooling effect. But weather is so variable anyway that some small effect is often difficult to see.

Could you give me some information about auroras?

Renee Leach
Baltimore, Maryland

An aurora is a wavering glow of light that is seen sometimes in the night sky in the direction of the North or South poles. The ones we see in the Northern Hemisphere are sometimes also called the northern lights.

An aurora is caused by very fast, charged particles—mostly electrons—that came from the Sun. Because of the earth's magnetic field, these are partially deflected so that they come into our atmosphere toward the North and South poles. When nitrogen molecules of our air are hit by those fast particles, they become very excited molecules.

They become ordinary molecules again by giving off energy as light. That gives the faint wavering glow we call an aurora.

I have little stickers that glow in the dark after the light goes off. How do they do that?

Christopher Dial
Talent, Oregon

There are a number of chemicals that are special in the way they react with light. They have molecules that take up light particles, or photons. They become "excited" molecules because they are holding extra energy that came from the photons. Later in time, they lose their "excitement" by giving off photons. Then they are giving off light and glowing.

For some molecules, photons are given off very quickly, even in billionths of a second. Such a very fast glow is called **fluorescence**. Some molecules hold on to their photon energy for a much longer time, even for hours. That slow glow is often called **phosphorescence**. You can see that fast and slow glows are much alike. Your stickers must contain some phosphorescent material.

One place that's easy to see phosphorescence is in a fluorescent lamp. It works mostly by a very fast glow of chemicals on the inside of the glass. But some of those chemicals also have a slow glow. A way to see this is to watch a fluorescent lamp in a dark room as you flip the light switch to turn it off. You will see that it glows a little after you turn off the switch.

What makes it snow?

Stephanie Waters
Indiantown, Florida

Snow forms in clouds when the air temperature up there gets below freezing. Water molecules come out of the air and stick together in special patterns of little ice crystals. Then the ice crystals keep getting bigger or tangle up in little clumps to form snowflakes.

Snowflakes have very intricate crystal patterns. There was a scientist who learned how to catch snowflakes and keep them cold long enough to take photographs. He photographed more than a thousand snowflakes without finding any two that were exactly alike. The scientist was called "Snowflake" Bentley.

Now that you know what snow is made of, let's hope we don't see too much of it at any one time.

How come snow is white?

Susannah Elwyn
Horseheads, New York

Why is snow white? The technical answer is that snow reflects most of the light that falls on it and it reflects all colors equally. You know that liquid water is clear and so nearly colorless that you can look right through it. That's also true of ice if it is made from pure water and has no cracks. If you scrape some ice, maybe with a knife or with your skates, you will see that scrapings are white and look something like snow. Just as with scraped ice, snow crystals scatter light rays and bounce them back without absorbing much. Since the snow doesn't absorb any color, we say that it is white.

How does a compass know where to point? How does it know the right direction?

Jennifer Pineda
Quartz Hill, California

A compass, as you know, has a small needle-like magnet for a pointer. Because the earth is a big magnet, the pointer-magnet of a compass lines up with the earth's magnetic field. So, the needle points almost north and south.

However, the earth's magnetic north pole is not exactly at the true North Pole. There are also small changes from place to place in the magnetic declination, how far off the compass will be from pointing true north.

If you want to know how to correct the compass in your area, I suggest you ask your local surveyor. He can tell you the proper declination to use.

In winter, every morning I look out the window and it's foggy. What causes that?

Timothy Manglona
San Diego, California

Fog forms when moist air is cooled a little. Then the water vapor condenses to make the many tiny droplets of water.

In some places the special conditions needed to make fog are likely to occur at certain times of year.

You live in San Diego, near the Pacific coast. I think your fogs occur when warm moist air from the ocean blows in over cooler water near shore.

I can't understand why clouds are white.

Jon Miller
Krum, Texas

It happens that I wrote an answer to that question when I answered Susannah Elwyn, who asked why snow is white. When I wrote Susannah's answer, I was not thinking about clouds, but clouds and snow are white for the same reason. They reflect most of the light that falls on them, and they reflect all colors equally.

What makes it rain?

Kim Scott
Snellville, Georgia

Rain always comes from a cloud. But, as you know, something special must happen in a cloud to make rain. Most clouds are made of water droplets so small that they are easily held up by very weak air currents.

In order to make rain, something has to happen to collect many tiny droplets into big drops, big enough to fall. One way this can happen is when there is a strong updraft. As it rises, the air expands and cools. In the churning air near the top of the cloud there are lots of collisions between droplets. Bigger droplets keep picking up smaller ones until they become raindrops big enough to fall.

Sometimes, if it gets cold enough in the cloud, ice crystals form. If they grow big enough to fall, they collect water droplets and may melt on the way down.

A lot has to happen up there in a cloud to make rain. Something has to turn many tiny floating droplets into large falling raindrops.

How does the oil on water change different colors like a rainbow? Is it because of the light reflections? Could you please explain it?

Courtney Pavelka
Denver, Colorado

That is an interesting sight that almost everyone sees sometime. An oil layer on water may spread out until it is very thin. When it gets to a particular thinness (or thickness), something special happens.

The water surface acts partly like a mirror and reflects back some of the light falling on it. An added oil layer now gives two partial mirrors very close together. When the distance between the mirrors is the same as the wave length of light, then those light waves cancel each other out. Then you see all the other wave lengths. Different wave lengths of light have different colors. So, you can say that the thin double mirror of an oil film on water actually erases some colors and leaves the others for you to see.

Sometimes I see a large, rainbow-like ring around the Moon and Sun. What causes this ring? I've been wondering for some time now.

Kathy Sue Brown
San Diego, California

That ring is sometimes called a halo. It is believed to be caused by the scattering of sunlight by tiny ice crystals very high in the sky.

High clouds of ice crystals high in the sky are called cirrus clouds, or cirrostratus if they form a layer. These often form in front of warm fronts that bring rain.

So, a halo around the Sun or Moon is often a warning that rain may come.

This afternoon I looked up and saw a rainbow moving back and forth across the wall. My mom said the sun goes to the fish tank and the sun in the fish tank goes to the wall. I don't believe her. What really happened?

Erica Martin
Tempe, Arizona

I think your mother is right. Here is what probably happened. A narrow band or sunlight fell upon your fish tank near one corner. Then the glass and water acted like a prism to break up the white light of sunlight into its colors.

I will show you by a diagram what a prism does. You can see how a corner of your fish tank could have done the same thing. I am sure you have noticed by now that everything has to be just right with the sun at a special angle to make a corner of your fish tank act like a prism.

It takes a little while to get used to the idea that you get from the rainbow of colors made by a prism. It shows you that white light is white because it contains all colors.

What makes the Sun and Moon shine?

Julie Blackwell
Bemis, Tennessee

Isn't it funny how we take such things for granted without ever knowing what causes them?

The Sun shines with its own energy. The light you see (and feel as heat) is given off by the Sun's surface, called the **photosphere**, which is several hundred miles thick and composed of ever-changing gases. Some of the energy the Sun produces must escape, or it would build up and explode. Whenever you see the Sun shining, you'll know it's just releasing excess energy and giving us a little light and warmth in the bargain.

Remember, you should never look directly at the Sun. The light is too bright for our eyes to take.

You also asked about moonshine. The Moon gives off no light of its own but reflects sunlight from its rocky surface. What we call moonshine is actually sunshine reflected by the Moon.

Did you know that there's also a third kind of shine? It's called earthshine, meaning sunlight reflected by the Earth. We have only one way to see it. That occurs because some of the earthshine falls on the Moon and is reflected back to Earth again. By this dim light we can sometimes see the outline of the whole moon behind the crescent of a new moon.

Why is the Moon dark when it moves in front of the Sun during an eclipse?

Tracy Stevens
Poquoson, Virginia

You see an eclipse of the Sun only at some special time when the Moon gets between the Sun and the place where you are standing on Earth. Then you are in the Moon's shadow.

If you think about this some more, you will see that the back side of the Moon, the side toward you, will also be in the same shadow. So, it will always look dark.

Why is there a leap year every four years?

Kecia Sinclair
St. Albans, New York

Your question got me thinking about how complicated the calendar really is. Maybe you would like to think about this, too.

Our Earth travels around the Sun in a very steady way. We use that to measure time in days.

Our Earth has another regular motion in its orbit around the Sun. Along with this motion we get the seasons of the year, which repeat themselves over and over. So, we also like to think in longer time periods measured in years.

It's easy to see why people chose days and years to keep time. But right away they had a problem because the number of days in a year does not come out even. There are about 365¼ days in a year.

Now you can see the idea of a leap year, which was invented way back at the time of Julius Caesar. If we put in one extra day every four years, that will keep us about even.

Actually, adding leap years is not a perfect solution. A real year is about 11 minutes and 14 seconds shorter than 365 1/4 days. Do you know how our calendar solves this problem? If you don't, try finding out in your school library. Look up calendars. And you may also be amazed to discover how many different calendars the different peoples of the world have invented.

Every year in the calendar a day starts on another space. For example, in 1983 the month of January started on a Sunday. In 1984 it started on a Monday. How come? Also, if one year January started on Saturday, on what day would January start on next year?

Erika Munos
West New York, New Jersey

Our calendar came about through many centuries of trying to find the best system. The ideas that went into it have been traced back to the ancient Egyptians, Mesopotamians, and Romans. The Mesopotamians may have been the ones who decided that the week should have seven days.

Our week still has seven days. And, as you know, our year has 365 days (except 366 days in leap years). If you divide 7 days into 365 days, you get 52 weeks in a year with *one day left over*. So, if January 1983 started on a Sunday, then January 1984 must have begun one day later—on Monday.

Now here's a question for you. 1984 was a leap year. So what day of the week did January 1985 begin on?

Why are there constellations?

Michelle Trautman
Scotts Valley, California

I'm not just sure how to answer your question. You did not ask why there are stars. Really, I think you want to know why people invented certain patterns out of the stars that we know as constellations.

A few thousand years ago life was a lot simpler. People generally lived by the Sun and worked during the daylight hours. At night lighting by candles or oil lamps was expensive. I suppose that people spent many evenings talking with their friends.

One of the ways to pass the time at night is to look at the stars. If you look at the night sky long enough, you can easily imagine that the star patterns look like the figures of animals or people. And if you let your imagination run, you can make up stories about them. I think that's how the constellations got their names.

We know that most of the star patterns came to be named as constellations. Those same names have been used for several thousands of years.

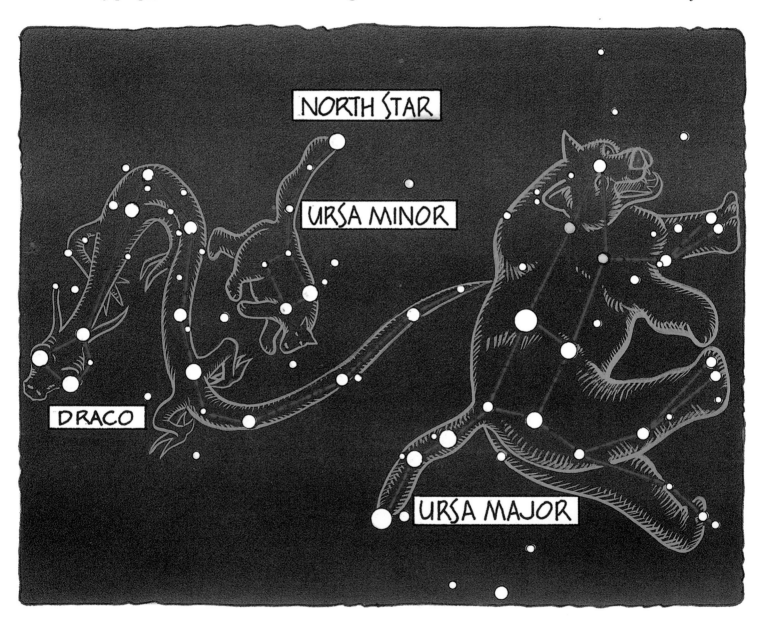

At night in the summer I look up at the stars and wonder what they are made of. I just keep wondering what they are made of. Could you please help me find out?

Rebecca Surratt
Atlanta, Texas

The stars are very great balls of very hot gas, mostly hydrogen and helium. Most of them are very much like our Sun.

So, when you look up at the stars at night, you can think of them as many suns looking so small because they are so far away.

How can we tell the temperature of stars?

Douglas Licerio
Palawan, Philippines

When we heat up something until it glows, we often say that it gets "red-hot." If we can make it still hotter, its color changes toward yellow, and still hotter, it becomes bluish white. So, you can see how we can tell about the temperature of something that glows like a star.

I found actual estimates of some star temperatures, given in the Centigrade temperature scale. Some of the bluish stars are about 40,000 degrees, and some of the reddish stars are only about 2,000 degrees. Our Sun is about 5,800 degrees. Of course, these are temperatures at the surface, which is the only part we can see.

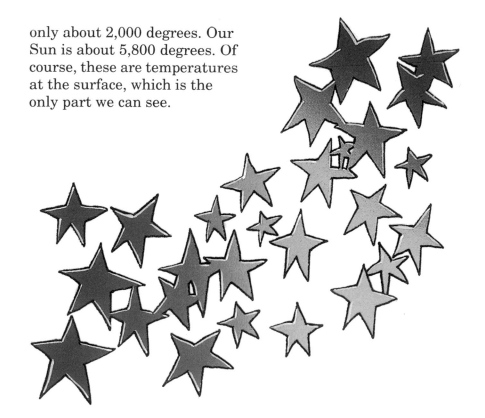

Why isn't there any air on the Moon?

Cassidy Wald
Red Deer, Alberta

That's a good question. We don't know exactly how the Moon was formed, but its composition, the stuff that makes it up, seems to be like that of the Earth. So, why no atmosphere?

The answer is that the Moon just doesn't have enough gravity to hold onto an atmosphere. Its force of gravity is only about one-ninth of that on Earth.

The force of gravity of the Earth is great enough to hold onto the gases of our atmosphere—except for the very lightest gases, hydrogen and helium. At the upper part of the Earth's atmosphere some of these two gases are continually being lost into space. So there are only tiny amounts of them left.

The Moon's gravity isn't great enough to hold any of the common gases. So, it's just a big naked ball out there without any atmosphere for clothes.

What do aliens from outer space look like?

Hank Williams, Jr.
Kokomo, Indiana

Let me help you think about your question. There may be some kind of life in other solar systems. However, if by outer space you mean within our solar system, I think you should know that scientists conclude there is not intelligent life with that system. There are people who wonder, of course, if other solar systems may have life and if that life might be similar to humans on planet Earth. We just don't know. It would be fun to think about what that life might look like. If you thought about humans and had a chance to start over, how would *you* make them different? Might there be some intelligent life that lived totally underwater? Or that could fly?

Lots of imaginative people draw pictures of aliens from outer space. You have seen some of these on TV and in magazines. These creatures are just people's guesses from within their imagination. What would your pictures look like?

I understand the meteors are pieces of metal that fly through space. But what I don't understand is how the metal gets into space. Could you explain that?

Joshua Graml
Langley AFB, Virginia

It seems that there are many little pieces of stone or metal that keep raining down on the Earth from out in space. They come down at very high speeds and get very hot as they are slowed by the friction of the atmosphere. They get hot enough to glow. Those that are big enough, maybe the size of a pea, make a trail of light that we call a **meteor**, or shooting star. Some of the larger pieces fall all the way to earth, and some are later found as pieces of metal or stone. These are called **meteorites**.

There really are many such particles that keep coming down all the time. Anyone who patiently watches the dark sky for several hours at night (and is away from city lights) should see several shooting stars. And sometimes there are so many that they are called meteor showers. Some are believed to come from stray pieces left over from comets. There are several different ideas about just where the larger ones come from, but they are believed to be pieces that belong to our solar system.

I guess that a lot of junk must be floating around out there in space.

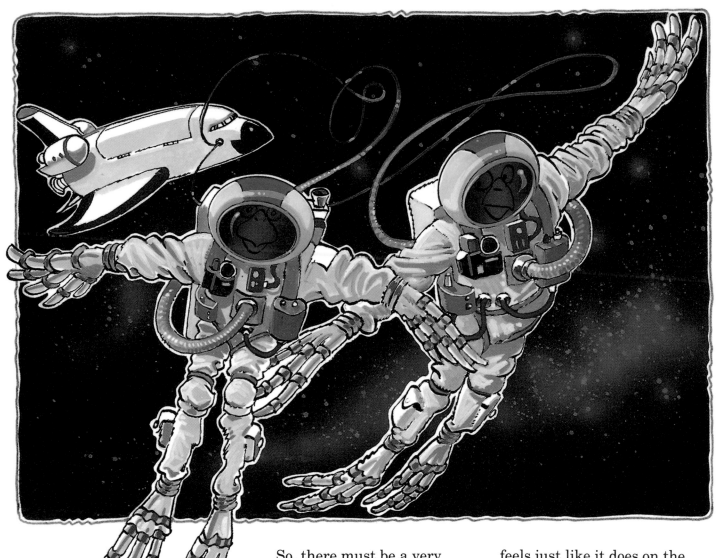

Why don't birds fly into space?

Meghan Chase
Casselberry, Florida

Your question starts from a correct idea. Birds do not fly out into space. In fact, I think it is safe to say that, in all the millions of years our Earth has had birds, we have never lost a bird that way.

So, there must be a very powerful reason why that cannot happen. Actually, there are several reasons. Let's think about two.

Some birds can fly pretty high up. I was surprised to read that some can fly as high as four miles above the earth. I am surprised because at that height the air is very thin. There are only half as many oxygen molecules in each breath of air. So, breathing is hard to do. Of course, airplanes carry people higher than that every day. But they have air pumps to pressurize the plane's cabin so that breathing feels just like it does on the ground.

Now you can see one problem. As a bird flies higher, the air gets thinner. A bird will run out of oxygen long before it gets out into space. And if a bird can't breathe, it can't fly.

There is also a second reason. In order for anything to really "escape" from the earth and get out into space, it needs a very great push in order to get up enough speed. The magic speed needed is called the escape velocity. It is about 25,000 miles per hour. You know that is a lot faster than a bird can fly.

This might seem difficult, but does sound travel in space?

Rachelle Theisen
Fargo, North Dakota

Sound is carried as a wave of compression in some material. The sounds we usually hear are carried by air.

Space is close to a perfect vacuum, meaning there's almost nothing there.
So, sound does not travel in space. There is no sense in yelling at a star.

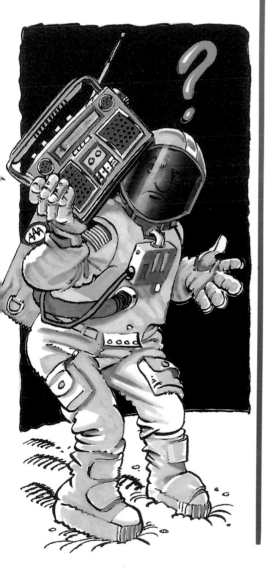

I know that there is another planet out there, but I don't know about it. Do you know anything about it?

Michelle Niehaus
Cincinnati, Ohio

The last planet to be discovered was Pluto. That happened in 1930. Astronomers had been looking for it for a long time. The reason to suspect another planet was that there were small changes in the orbits of Uranus and Neptune that could have been caused by the effect of gravity of an unknown planet.

Lately I have noticed questions about whether the mass of Pluto is really great enough to cause those effects on Uranus and Neptune. So, maybe it is possible that there is still another planet way out on the edge of our solar system. Most astronomers, it seems, don't believe that, but I guess we'll just have to wait and see.

How do birds communicate?

Maria Spredbury
FPO, New York

I think most birds communicate by making sounds. There are a large number of sounds made by different species. Some of these are songs. Many more are simpler sounds, like cheeps and quacks and caws and twitters. Birds cannot talk and express ideas the way you and I do, but they can send some simple messages, like "This is my territory," or "Danger, danger," or "I like you."

Some birds communicate also by displays, as a male turkey does when it ruffs up its feathers. I think such displays are usually used in mating.

Animal communication is a big subject for research, so we are learning more all the time.

I have made a birdhouse, but not a bird touches it. I put bird seed in it and mud and grass, but still not a bird goes into it. Could you help me?

Ellie Mendenhall
Omaha, Nebraska

You could try reading about the kinds of birds that live in Nebraska. Find out what kinds of places they like to live and what kinds of food they like to eat. That may help you to place your birdhouse where a bird will be more likely to use it.

Not all kinds of birds like to use birdhouses. And some kinds are very particular. I think little wrens will use only birdhouses with very small holes for openings.

Also, you will find that where you put a birdhouse is important. Birds usually are careful to nest where cats and snakes and squirrels will not be a problem. Birds build their own nests, and each kind does that in its own way. So, I think it may not be a good idea to put grass and mud in it.

My best suggestion is this. Look around town and see who has birdhouses with birds. Then go ask those people for their advice. It will be better than mine.

Once my mom cracked open an egg, and there were two yolks. Can there be two chickens in one egg?

Devon Greyson
Ann Arbor, Michigan

No. Or at least it's not very likely. One reason is that there probably is not enough stored food in the egg to allow two chicks to develop. And I have never found anyone who has actually seen two chicks hatch from one egg.

How do baby birds breathe inside their eggs?

Nora Mahlberg
Madison, Wisconsin

I'm glad that you are wondering about some of the many interesting things you see in nature.

A bird's eggshell and the lining inside are very neat inventions. As you know, a baby bird has to start growing up while still inside the egg. The eggshell is good at holding water in so the insides don't dry up. And it allows the gases oxygen and carbon dioxide to seep through. That's how the baby bird does its breathing before it gets big enough to break out of the shell.

I live on a ranch. When we have to pull a calf out of the cow, it has a "sack" of phlegm or something. Why is it there? I know colts have it, too.

Lane Buchanan
Baggs, Wyoming

I have never actually seen a calf pulled out of a cow at birth. So you know more about this than I do, and I am not sure about what you call a "sack" of phlegm. Maybe what I can tell you will help.

In most mammals the birth process is pretty standard, at least in principle. The baby has developed in the uterus of the mother. It is attached to the wall of the uterus by a special tissue, the placenta. And it is enclosed in two surrounding, fluid-filled sacs.

In squeezing its way out of the uterus, the sac must break. The baby is born still attached by a cord to the placenta. In some way the cord is cut or broken. Then afterwards the placenta, usually called the afterbirth, breaks loose and is also discharged.

All those same things will happen when a baby is born, whether in humans, or cows, or horses. I hope this will help you answer your question.

I would like to know about snakes. How do snakes make babies?

Franco Tassone
LaSalle, Quebec

The egg cells of female snakes must be fertilized before they can have babies or lay eggs that will hatch. You may know that some snakes keep the eggs inside and have babies inside their bodies. Others lay their eggs outside. Rattlesnakes, copperheads, moccasins, and garter snakes have babies. Sometimes they have very large families. A snake may have nearly one hundred babies at one time.

Bullsnakes, rat snakes, racers, pythons, and many others lay eggs. One python once laid more than one hundred. How would you like to have a hen that laid this many eggs at one time? Snake eggs are quite different from the eggs of birds and chickens. They have a different shape, and the shell is not easy to break, like that of a chicken's eggs. The shell of a snake's egg is tough and leathery.

O.P.B.

I would like to learn more about the poisonous snakes in the world. The ones I am really interested in are rattlesnakes because my family owns a cabin in the Poconos.

William Sandor
Easton, Pennsylvania

There are several kinds of snakes that are called vipers. Rattlesnakes, copperheads, and the cottonmouth moccasin belong to a group called pit vipers. They get that name because all of them have a small pit or depression between the eye and the nostril on each side. These pits are heat detectors. They help the snake find a smaller animal, such as a mouse, even at night. The pit vipers are poisonous.

There are a dozen or so different kinds of rattlesnakes, most of which live in the southern parts of the United States. I have not had much experience in Pennsylvania. There is a rattler called the massasauga, or swamp rattler, reported from Pennsylvania, and I think also the timber rattler. The copperhead also occurs in Pennsylvania, but none of the other pit vipers.

One is not nearly as likely to find a poisonous snake in Pennsylvania as in many of the southern states. However, when you are in the woods, or walking through the high grass or weeds, you should take some precautions. Don't step over a log until you can see the ground on the other side, and always look before you step. If a rock or log is moved, you should stand well to one side until you can see what is under it. And, of course, you should never stick your hand in a hole in the ground or in a cavity in a tree.

When walking in high grass or weeds, push a stick in front of you before you step. Most poisonous snakes in the United States will crawl away rather than bite, if you give them the chance. Incidentally, as I can tell you from experience, rattlesnakes do not always rattle before they strike.

O.P.B.

I have a question. Do bumblebees make honey?

Jacob Delph
Phoenix, Arizona

Bumblebees are usually yellow and black, larger than honeybees, and look even larger because of a thick covering of hair. Bumblebees do make honey, but only enough to live on during the summer. They are social, which means that many bees live together in a colony.

Usually they live underground, maybe in an old nest left by a field mouse. In a colony there are different kinds, like drones and workers and queens, but they are not as well organized as honeybees.

At least in the northern states, only a few queens live through the winter by finding hiding places in the ground. So, they do not have to make a big store of honey to feed the whole colony during the winter.

When I think about bumblebees, I think of a story often told by my father. He grew up on a farm in southern Pennsylvania. When he was old enough, he was taught to plow. The plow was pulled by a horse or team of horses. The driver walked behind the plow and held onto its two handles to keep it pointed right as it turned over the soil. My father used a big and strong but very slow horse called Kate. The very worst thing that could happen was that the plow would go through a bumblebee nest. Then Kate would stop and stamp her feet. And my father was stuck with a lot of very mad bumblebees. You can see why my father never forgot that experience, even when he became the first editor of HIGHLIGHTS many years later.

30

How can you tell a butterfly from a moth?

Andy Strain
Brownsburg, Indiana

Moths and butterflies are much alike, and they are classified into the same group or order. The order name is Lepidoptera, which means "scaly wings." The reason for the name is that both moths and butterflies have scales on their wings and bodies. But moths and butterflies do have some differences.

Both moths and butterflies have two projections—called antennae, or "feelers"—from their heads. The antennae of butterflies are enlarged at the tips into small clubs. The antennae of moths are of different kinds, some hairlike and feathery, but they do not have clubs at the tips.

When butterflies are at rest, they hold their wings straight above them. Moths at rest usually hold their wings flat on each side of their bodies.

Butterflies fly during the day, and moths fly mostly at night. The ones you see flying among the flowers during the day are butterflies. Those you see flying around lights at night are moths.

O.P.B.

I have a pet turtle that hibernates in the winter. I went to school and asked the kids at school if turtles hibernate. They said that they don't. Is that true or false?

Theresa Bauccio
St. Louis, Missouri

You know very well what your turtle does. I suppose it just gets into a dark place and stays there. The question is whether that is really hibernation.

Zoologists have come to use the word *hibernation* in a special way. Technically, it applies to just a few animals, mostly mammals, that control their body temperature. During hibernation they lower their temperatures and turn down their body machinery.

Cold-blooded animals, those that do not control their body temperatures, can't just slow down their machinery that way. But many do go dormant, stay quiet, and maybe not eat anything for long periods. Many reptiles do that. So, if there is an argument, it is only about what the word *hibernation* really means.

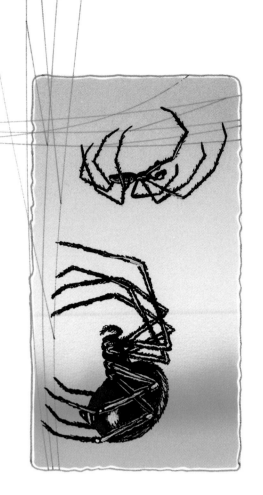

How can you tell the difference between a male and a female black widow spider?

Mindy Camls
Grand Prairie, Texas

Because George Frame recently wrote me about watching black widow spiders, I thought he could answer your question better than I could. Here is what he said.

"It isn't easy to see if a spider is a male or a female. Young spiders of both sexes look alike, but as they grow to adult size, some differences appear.

"The male black widow spider has a thinner body than does the female. The adult male black widow spider (and the male of many other kinds of spiders, too) is smaller than the adult female.

"All spiders have one pair of short 'arms' (called pedipalps) in front of their four pairs of long legs. The 'arms' of an adult male spider are always thick. Only young males and all females (young or adult) have thin 'arms.' Some people say that adult male spiders look like they are wearing boxing gloves.

"The black widow spider got its name because the adult female sometimes kills and eats her mate. If she is well fed, the male usually is not harmed."

I recently went to the zoo and saw a green polar bear. What causes it to turn green?

Aviva Pollack
San Diego, California

This happens in zoos if there are algae growing in pools of water where polar bears splash around. Some of the tiny cells of algae get into the hollow hairs of the bears and grow there. That makes the bears look green.

I think this discovery of why white polar bears become green was first made in your San Diego zoo. And it was made by a friend of mine, Dr. Ralph Lewin, who likes to look for algae growing in strange places.

As far as I can find, reports of green polar bears come only from zoos. I doubt that there are any green polar bears swimming in the Arctic Ocean.

Can you tell a male frog from a female frog? If so, how?

Becky Cable
Dallas, Texas

There is no easy way to tell a male from a female frog unless the frog is croaking or "singing." Any frog that croaks or sings is a male. Female frogs may make small sounds if they are injured or bothered, but females never sing or croak for long periods around ponds or streams, as males often do. The songs of male frogs attract the females to them during the mating season.

Another way to tell a male from a female frog is to look in the frog's mouth. Male frogs and toads have vocal sacs, or resonating chambers, that cause the songs to be louder. The openings of these vocal sacs are in the mouth, and they are in different places in frogs and toads. In common frogs, such as the leopard frog, these openings, one on each side, are in the rear part of the lower jaw near where the two jaws are hinged together. In toads, the openings to the vocal sacs are two slits in the lower jaw, one on each side of the tongue.

When male frogs and toads sing, they take air into their vocal sacs. This air causes the vocal sacs to get much bigger so that they can be seen. In frogs there are two vocal sacs, one on each side of the body. When filled with air, these sacs bulge out the body wall just behind the eye. In toads, there is one vocal sac under the lower jaw or throat. When a male toad is singing, the vocal sac sometimes gets so big that it looks like a large rounded sack to which a small toad is attached.

O.P.B.

Why do giraffes have long necks?

Lisa Marse
Metairie, Louisiana

The question *why?* is often very difficult and sometimes impossible to answer. Another question that you may be thinking about is: How did we get animals like giraffes that have such long necks?

That does seem a puzzle, and no one can tell you exactly how that happened. I have supposed that it happened this way. Way back in time, millions of years ago, there were plant-eating animals that learned to reach up in the trees for food. The higher they could reach, the better, because then they could eat juicy leaves that other animals could not reach. Taller giraffes had an advantage because they could reach higher. They had more to eat, they were stronger, and they had more babies. That meant the giraffes kept getting taller, or got longer necks, because that kind always had the advantage.

I think you can see how that could happen. Of course, I cannot prove to you that it happened this way. But no one has told me a more sensible explanation.

You will learn more about things like this as you study biology. The long neck of the giraffe is a curiosity. But almost every animal has something special or peculiar about it, and you can wonder how it got that way.

Though fleas jump, and do not fly, do they have wings?

Christa Gormley
Bloomington, Indiana

Fleas do not have wings, but they can easily get around because they are great jumpers. I think that for their size, fleas are the champion jumpers among the insects. A person who could jump as well as the best flea jumper could probably jump over the Washington Monument.

Fleas live on birds and mammals. They are a nuisance because they bite. Actually they are more than just a nuisance because they can carry diseases from one animal to another. One disease carried among rats and also from rats to people is called bubonic plague. Many years ago (especially in the years 1347 to 1351, if you like numbers) it was the worst disease in all of Europe and killed almost a third of the people. Bubonic plague is no longer as common. Today we know how the disease is carried. And good medical treatments are known.

If there are fleas in a house, they probably were brought in by pet dogs or cats. If people have fleas in a house or yard, they should ask a veterinarian how to get rid of them.

O.P.B.

Why can't rabbits make sounds?

Eric Dodson
Niles, Ohio

Actually rabbits can make sounds, but they seldom do. I do not really know why.

People who have had long experience with rabbits say that the animals sometimes make low grunting noises. They believe that the grunting noises mean that the rabbits are pleased. Also, tame rabbits will sometimes thump their hind legs on the floor of the cage. It is believed that these sounds are meant to be warnings of possible danger. People who spend a lot of time in the wild have told me that an injured or wounded rabbit will sometimes squeal or scream.

There are many different kinds of rabbits in the United States, and it may be that some kinds make more noises than others. According to one report, Indians in the northern parts of the United States and in Canada often attracted snowshoe rabbits to them by making squeaking sounds. This trick worked only during the mating season, and it may be that during this time rabbits make these sounds to attract other rabbits. I do not know if this method of attracting snowshoe rabbits is still used.

O.P.B.

Why do crickets chirp? I think they do it to put other animals to sleep. Is that true? And why at night?

Marie Aquino
West Paterson, New Jersey

I think there probably are two reasons why crickets chirp. At least in most kinds of crickets, the chirping is done by the males. The chirping is a kind of mating call and helps a female find the male. Also, it probably serves as a warning to other males to stay away.

As you say, most cricket chirping occurs at night. I cannot really say why except that most crickets seem to be nocturnal, or night-loving, animals.

Flying fish don't really fly, do they?

Jody Schmidt
DePere, Wisconsin

Flying fish are certainly among the most interesting sights that one is likely to see on an ocean voyage. Suddenly the little fish break the water surface and go sailing away like so many streaks of light.

The questions most often asked about flying fish are: how do they get out of the water, and do they actually fly?

The "wings" of the flying fish are the front fins, which are greatly enlarged. The fish gets into the air by swimming very rapidly near the water surface by strong movements of the tail. Suddenly the fish comes to the surface, spreads the front fins, and holds them rigid. The fins act like the wings of a glider; they lift the fish into the air, and keep it there as it goes sailing over the waves. Flying fish may stay in the air for several hundred yards, and sometimes they get so high that they land on the decks of large ships.

At one time it was thought that a flying fish actually flew by flapping its fins as a bird does its wings, but it is now known that the fins are held rigid and not flapped. Thus flying fish do not actually fly like birds, but they sail, or glide, like gliders.

O.P.B.

When ice freezes, how do dolphins breathe? I know they're mammals but they are in the water. They also need to breathe, though.

Melissa Stewart
Vincennes, Indiana

You asked that question because you know that dolphins are mammals. They can't get oxygen from water the way fish do. So, they have to come to the surface often to breathe air.

The answer is that dolphins don't live where the ocean freezes over, as it does close to the North and South poles. They live in the warmer oceans that never freeze over.

Would you please explain why the so-called Jack Frost pictures and designs get to be on our windows?

Laurie Ann Boast
Noranda, Quebec

You can see that the frost on a window is always on the inside. And if the outside temperature warms up, or maybe if a window is right in the sun, the frost may melt into water that runs down on the inside of the window. So, you can see that the frost is made out of ice that formed on the inside of the window.

Frost forms on a window when the temperature outside is below freezing. Inside it is warmer, and there is more water vapor in the air. Any water molecule in the air that hits the glass will stick to the surface. As it sticks, it is hooking up to other water molecules to form ice crystals.

Every water molecule is made of one oxygen and two hydrogen atoms, H-O-H. Water molecules can stick together by sharing their hydrogen atoms. They tend to make six-sided shapes but in all kinds of patterns. The really amazing thing about frost on windows is that it forms in such varied and beautiful patterns. If you were wondering why they make some of the particular Jack Frost patterns, I just have to say that I do not know.

I have been thinking that Jack Frost patterns on windows must be common where you live in Canada. That led me to think also that some people have never seen them.

37

Which is faster, heat or cold?

Sandy Wolf
Orlando, Florida

When we talk about things around us, we commonly say that something (like boiling water) is hot and something else (like an ice cube) is cold. Sometimes we even use a thermometer that measures in degrees how hot or cold something is.

When we want to think about making something hot, we can think about adding *heat* to it or taking *cold* away from it. Really, those two ways of

thinking would be exactly the same. So, the answer to your question would be: heat is just as fast as cold.

Actually, we do not use the ideas of cold in this way. All we need to think about is heat. We make something hot by adding heat. That's what a fire can do. We make something cold by taking heat away from it. That's what a refrigerator can do.

A lot of different conditions affect how fast you can add heat to make something hot. They work in just the same way to affect how fast you can take heat away to make something cold.

How's that for a hot idea?

How does temperature change?

Kimmy Jones
Coon Rapids, Minnesota

Our Earth is warmed by the Sun. But it is not warmed evenly. We have some places, like the poles, that get the least sunshine and are always cold. And we have a big central band near the equator that gets the most sunshine and is usually hot. With air rising where it is hot and settling down where it is cool, there are bound to be winds in between. With things like oceans and land and lakes and mountains in between, the winds get mixed up a lot. Wherever we are, the winds do not always come from the same place. So, the temperature of the air around us can change a great deal.

We have learned a lot about our weather by studying the movement of air. The scientists who do that are called meteorologists. They usually can tell pretty well what the weather will be like. But they are never quite certain because it is hard to tell just how the winds will blow tomorrow.

How come light is so hot?

Rhona Seidman
Silver Spring, Maryland

Light is a form of energy very different from heat. Light itself is not hot. However, we can *make* light with something that is hot enough. And we can use light to warm something and *make* heat. So, I can see why you might have asked your question.

Of all the ways to make light, the oldest is to get something very hot. When Edison started out to make an electric light bulb, that's the idea he used. He used electricity to heat a wire sealed up in a bulb. We still use that kind of light bulb. The outer bulb gets hot, but the wire inside is heated up much hotter—to almost 3000° F. However, there are other ways to make light without much heat. Our fluorescent lamps are warm but never really get hot. And a firefly makes "cold" light—no heat at all.

We are fortunate that light can be turned into heat and used to warm something. If it were not for sunlight, our Earth would be a frozen, lifeless planet. No heat travels across that 93,000,000 miles from the Sun. It is sunlight turned into heat that keeps us warm.

Just think of light and heat as different forms of energy that can be changed from one to the other.

I read that everything expands when it's heated. Would it shrink when it gets cold?

Randy Powell
Elmore City, Oklahoma

You are right that most things expand when they are heated. They also shrink when they get cold. So, we ought to be able to use this idea to tell what temperature it is.

That's what a thermometer does. The liquid inside expands up the tube at higher temperature and shrinks back down the tube at lower temperature. And it will keep on doing this day after day and year after year.

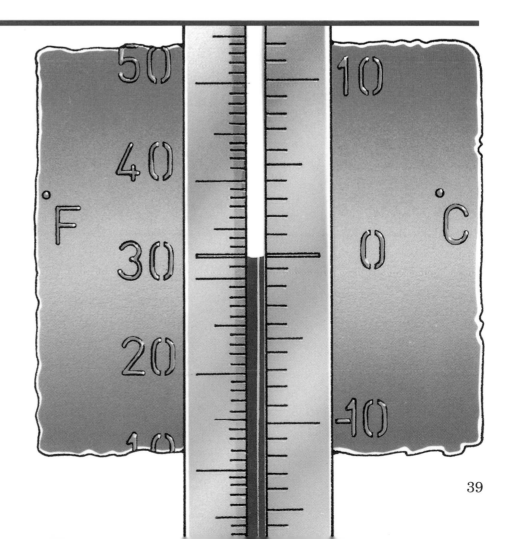

If there are more trees in the mountains than in the city, why is there more oxygen in the city than in the mountains?

Raudy Steele
Westcliffe, Colorado

You are correct that there is less oxygen in the air high in the mountains. But I think the rest of your idea is not quite right.

Cities are usually in valleys so that when you go to the mountains you go up higher. As you go higher, there is less air above you. So, there's less pressure from the air above squeezing on the air around you. A common way to say this is that as you go higher, the air around you gets thinner.

Getting thinner means that a quart of air has less air in it. That's why it has less oxygen.

How did Columbus prove the earth is round?

Karen Raplee
Pine City, New York

The idea that the earth is round seems to have been stated almost 2,000 years before Columbus. However, proving the idea was not as easy as it is today. Proving the idea so that everyone could understand it was even harder. After all, the earth does *seem* to be flat (except for its mountains and valleys). I suppose that at the time of Columbus, when very few people could even read and write, most people believed only what they could see and feel.

Columbus knew the earth had to be round. If that were true, then he could get to China in the east by sailing west. That meant sailing out across the Atlantic Ocean, where no one had ever gone before. And that took a lot of courage, especially since most people (including his sailors) thought he was crazy.

Of course, Columbus did not get all the way round the world, so you could say he didn't completely prove it was round. What he did do was to make it easier for everyone to understand the idea.

How do some people get to be scientists?

*Julie Morgan
Rockford, Illinois*

I do not know anyone who has all of the answers to this question, but I will tell you my ideas about it. The first idea is that people who become scientists are curious people. They wonder about the universe, or the world we live in, or about its people. And they wonder hard enough to want to find out. They like puzzles; they like to solve problems. In fact, they like to think.

A famous scientist, a physicist who worked at the Bell Laboratories, once asked me, "How many people ever really sit and think?" What he meant was that many people do not like questions unless someone else tells them the answers, or maybe he meant that many people are lazy in using their brains. I think that lazy-brain people would never become scientists.

Of course, no one will ever learn much about science just sitting on a desert island and thinking. We need to know the ideas about science that already are known, the ones that scientists before us have discovered. Galileo, who lived about 400 years ago, was one of the great scientists of all time. If you are in the fifth grade, you already know a great deal more about our world than Galileo did.

We also need to learn how to use the tools of science. Some tools are instruments, like microscopes or telescopes or computers. Learning to use them is a little like learning to drive a car. Some tools are just ways of thinking—like mathematics. Of course, mathematics is a special kind of science all by itself. But for most scientists, mathematics is their most powerful tool.

So if you have an idea that you might like to be a scientist, one bit of advice anyone will give is to study math. For some of us math is easy; for some of us it's hard. And when it is hard, it usually also seems dull. I was very poor in math until the eighth grade. I don't remember exactly what happened, but somehow I solved a problem all by myself. And suddenly I thought, "Gee, that was fun." After that I liked math, and I have learned to use it in my work, even though I never really got to be a good mathematician.

Suppose you work hard to learn about science and math and then later decide you don't want to be a scientist. Should you worry about that? Will your study be wasted? I don't think so. We live in a world that depends upon science and technology. The more you know about science, the more you will feel at home in the world you are growing up in.

When you write with a pencil, how does the lead work?

Jennifer Buttlar
Nashua, New Hampshire

The lead in your pencil is made out of graphite, a form of carbon, with some clay added in. About four hundred years ago when people learned to use graphite for writing, people supposed that it was a form of the element lead. So, the black stuff in the center of a pencil is still called the lead.

A pencil works to make marks on a paper because it is soft enough to rub off on the paper. It's also soft enough to scrape down to a point when you sharpen the pencil.

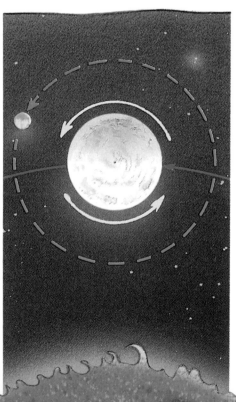

Where does the Sun go when the Moon comes out? Where does the Moon go when the Sun comes out? Does the Moon make night? Does the Sun make day? I don't know the answers, but I like day more.

Vicki Doucet
Bathurst, New Brunswick

The Sun is a hot glowing ball that gives us light and keeps us warm. Our Earth is revolving around the Sun like a big spinning ball. So, about half the time the Sun seems to be overhead and it is daytime. And about half the time the Sun is on the other side and it is night on our side.

The Moon is always making a big circle around the earth. We see it when it is only on our side of the earth. And we see it only in light that it reflects back to us from the Sun. Sometimes you can see the Moon during the daytime, but then it looks only a little brighter than the sky behind it.

The Moon looks best when we see it at night. Then it looks very bright against the dark sky.

What are diamonds made of?

*Kristi Ann Garatti
Thunder Bay, Ontario*

Diamonds are made out of the element carbon. So, all the atoms in a diamond are alike. Each one is bonded to four neighboring carbons, each exactly the same distance away. Once they get put together that way, it is very difficult to move them around. So, a diamond is one of the hardest substances we have.

There are other ways to put carbon atoms together. So, we have other substances—like charcoal and lampblack and graphite—also made out of carbon. Chemists like to talk about these different forms of carbon. They show that even when substances are made from just one kind of atom, their properties depend on the way the atoms are hooked together.

What are chemicals made of?

*Jason Creppel
Harvey, Louisiana*

One answer is that chemicals are made out of molecules, tiny particles way too small to see even with a microscope. There are many different kinds of molecules. Each kind is made out of a particular combination of atoms. An atom is the smallest particle of an element and there are more than 100 different kinds of elements.

What I have just said is true about any substance you can think of—rocks and dirt and wood and even your body. But when you talk about a chemical, you usually think of a pure substance made out of just one kind of molecule.

One chemical you see in almost pure form every day is ordinary table salt. Each one of its molecules is made out of one atom of sodium and one atom of chlorine. So, its name is sodium chloride.

Now you can think like a chemist.

43

I have chosen the topic windmills for a science fair project. My question is: Are windmills still useful today?

Jamie White
West Bridgewater, Massachusetts

I hope you have learned a lot about windmills. They were invented over a thousand years ago, long before people had any steam or gas engines. A hard job that took a lot of work was the grinding of grain to make a kind of flour. It seems that grinding grain was the common work done by windmills in Europe for several hundred years. They are not used for that anymore because we have much better sources of energy, like electric and gasoline motors.

In the United States windmills came into wide use as a way of pumping water. There aren't so many anymore. It's easier and cheaper to use an electric motor than to repair a windmill. But there are still some working out West, mostly in lonely places without close-by electricity. I think you can still buy those windmills built like big fans and held up on steel towers.

Nowadays we are searching for sources of energy that don't depend on the burning of coal and oil. So, engineers are working with windmills again to see if they can make them good enough to generate electricity practically. Of course, wind (like sunlight) is free. But the trick is to build a windmill that will generate electricity cheaply and reliably.

I guess we have to say that, even though we now have other sources of energy, windmills are still useful.

Suppose you stopped at the stop sign. Is the gas used by the car being wasted?

Mary Haryan
Syracuse, New York

You are exactly right that the gasoline used by an automobile at a stop sign is being wasted. Trouble is, if the stop is only very brief, it is better to use this gas than to restart your car. That may not be true while waiting alongside a curb for a friend. I am glad you are thinking about the way we use gasoline.

What is compost, and what is it used for?

Kelly Stewart
Fairfield, Ohio

Compost can be made out of anything that will rot or decay.

It is commonly made out of grass clippings, leaves, or even garbage. It works in the same way as the recycling processes of nature.

Think of all the leaves that fall from trees every autumn. During the year they slowly just seem to disappear. We say that they decompose or rot or decay. What we mean is that they became food for the molds and bacteria of soil. Only some of their fibers are left to become a part of the soil and decay more slowly.

Composting uses the same idea but usually is done by piling stuff together, maybe in an open box. (Most people don't put meat scraps in compost mainly because decaying meat usually smells bad.) The compost that results is good fertilizer for gardens and lawns.

Do rocks grow?

David Dion
Framingham, Massachusetts

Do rocks grow? No, not in the sense that living things grow. Of course, when rocks were formed, or when they are being formed now, they are increasing in size. Think of a stalactite, which looks like a rock icicle hanging from the ceiling of a cave. It increases in size as ground water drips over it and leaves calcium carbonate behind, little by little.

You might say that it grows, but you will see that it really increases in size only by adding more of itself to its outside. Living things do not grow that way. An animal takes in food and changes the food to make more animal.

How do clouds float when there is gravity and feathers can't?

Sarah McMurray
Oxnard, California

I like your question. It shows that you are a good observer and curious about nature. And it isn't easy to see why clouds should be able to stay up when something as light as a feather can't.

A cloud is made out of jillions of tiny water droplets. Each droplet all by itself is too small for your eye to see. Each droplet is pulled toward the earth just like anything else.

But tiny particles have lots more surface compared to their weight. That gives a lot of friction in moving through air. Because of that they fall very slowly.

Even though they fall slowly, something else must work to keep cloud droplets from falling to the ground. What keeps them up there are upward-blowing drafts of air. If you have watched clouds, you have noticed that they are always changing in shape. They are always moving in those gusty winds that hold them up there.

You can see that it takes a lot of different ideas to understand why clouds behave the way they do.

Since there is gravity on both ends of the earth, would it be true that if someone dug a hole through the earth he could stay in the middle without falling through?

Jill Schmidt
Wichita, Kansas

I asked my friend Claude Horton to help answer your question. Here is his answer.

"We are used to thinking of falling toward the earth. What we call gravity is the attraction between the very great mass of the earth and the mass of another object, like your body.

"In talking about the gravitational force between two objects, we can treat each object as if its mass were concentrated at its very center.

"When we get inside the earth, as in a deep mine shaft, things get more complicated. Then an object is closer to the center of the earth, and we would expect the gravitational force toward the center to be even greater. But there is also some mass of earth nearer the surface that causes an upward force on the object. The result of these two attractions is a force toward the center of the earth, but it is smaller than the force at the surface.

"The easiest way to answer your question is to think about ideal conditions. This is a trick that physicists often use to make things as simple as possible. We will imagine that there is no friction, that your body never scrapes against the side of the hole, and that there is no air to slow down its motion. Then if you fell in, you would fall all the way through and come to the surface at the other end of the hole.

"Of course, you would fall right back again. If no one stopped your motion, you would oscillate forever, falling back and forth from one end of the hole to the other.

"If there is even a small amount of friction with air or by rubbing against the sides of the hole, the answer will be different. Then if you fell into the hole, you would never quite reach the other side. You would oscillate back and forth; but each travel would be shorter than the one before—like a swing dying down. In time you would come to rest right at the center of the earth.

"I am sure you understand that we have talked about a completely imaginary problem and not any real experiment. The center of the earth has a very hot liquid core, and no one thinks seriously of drilling a hole through it. And even if we could do such an experiment, I do not think you would want to fall in just to see if I am right."

Once I went to Yellowstone and saw geysers. I would like to know more about them.

Chris Haley
Cincinnati, Ohio

I am glad you got to see the Yellowstone geysers. As I remember, the Park Service there has a display showing how geysers work. The next time you are there, ask a park ranger to show you the geyser display.

There is a simple way to tell the idea of how a geyser works. It's something like a coffee percolator. There has to be a hot place down deep in the ground and some way for water to get down to it.

Geysers occur only where the hot molten interior of the earth comes close enough to the surface. That heats up the rocks down below. Water falling on the hot rock gets turned into steam, which expands with great force. That drives out steam and hot water. If there is a hole to the surface above and a cave that can hold part of the water running down, that gives the special formation needed to make a geyser.

I have not told you all about geysers, but maybe enough so you can see the idea of how they work.

Why doesn't a rubber band shoot underwater, and why doesn't a bubble sink in water?

Norman Kuong
Chicago, Illinois

A rubber band does not "shoot" very well underwater. This is because the water is thicker (denser) than air, so the water puts up more resistance. It's easy to notice that it is harder to push your hand through water than it is to wave your hand through the air.

A bubble of air is a lot lighter than the same volume of water. When a bubble is formed underwater, the much heavier water tries to take its place, and that pushes the bubble to the surface.

You may wonder why some bars of soap float on water and others sink. The companies that make their soap to float trap air inside the soap bar. That carries the soap to the top of the water.

I would like to know why water foams, like in a river when the water goes over a fall.

Laura Ernst
Stoughton, Massachusetts

I think foam is made by churning up water and getting some air bubbles in it. In very pure water the bubbles break very quickly. However, it is difficult to get very pure water, even in a chemistry laboratory. The difficulty is that so many things dissolve in water. Even in a mountain stream the water contains substances from rocks and soil and fish that help to make bubbles and some foam.

Of course, you know that some things, like soap, help to make water foam. So, streams that contain soaplike stuff are likely to be foamier. I think that if you could make a small river from the water of your bathtub it would be pretty foamy.

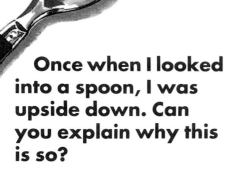

Once when I looked into a spoon, I was upside down. Can you explain why this is so?

Shan Scott
Oxon Hill, Maryland

The shiny surface of a spoon makes a good mirror for bouncing back, or reflecting, light rays. And the inside of a spoon has a cupped-in surface so that it is called a **concave** mirror. If you are far enough away from it, any concave mirror behaves just the way you described.

One common way to show how mirrors work is to use lines to describe the path of light rays and make a scale diagram. I will make such a diagram and will tell you what it means.

First I drew a part of a circle to represent the curved surface of the mirror. Then I drew the arrow AB to represent an *object*. I used an arrow only because it is easier to draw than a man. Then I drew in four light rays. The *a* lines start from A, the tip of the arrow, and the *b* lines start from B, the back end of the arrow. The upper *a* line strikes the mirror at an angle and is reflected back at an angle. The lower *a* line strikes the mirror head on and is reflected straight back. If you draw them correctly, all possible rays of light from A to the mirror will be reflected so that they pass through point A'. I drew only two of them to show the idea. Also, all possible rays of light from point B, like the *b* lines shown, will past through point B'.

An object like the arrow AB really is described by a large number of points, and we could draw more lines to show rays from many more of them. But just the lines from A and B are enough to show the idea: the convex mirror will form an image A'B' of the object AB.

In looking into a spoon, you are the object like the arrow AB, and you see yourself reflected like the image A'B'. Notice two things about the image in the diagram. First, it is smaller than the object. Secondly, it is inverted, or upside down. The image of yourself that you see in a spoon works the same way.

You might also notice how your image changes when you hold the spoon up and down or crosswise. One way you will look tall and skinny, the other way short and fat. Maybe you have already guessed why. The spoon has one curvature along it, and a different curvature across it. The inside of a spoon is really a very complex kind of concave mirror.

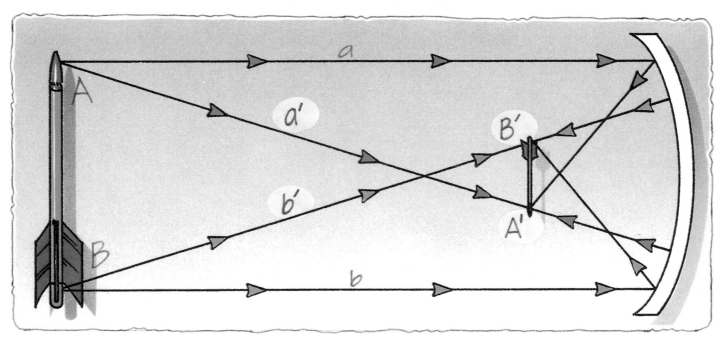

When a car is traveling forward, why do the wheels appear to be rotating backward?

Ben Leary
Donelson, Tennessee

That doesn't happen when you are looking directly at a real car. But it does occur sometimes when you see a car in the movies or on TV.

The effect occurs for the same reason in moving pictures and on TV: We are looking at a series of picture taken in rapid succession. Our eyes smear the successive pictures together so that we think we are seeing smooth and continuous motion. This works fine until we start to look at rapid repetitive motions like the spokes of a turning wheel.

The effect is easier for me to think about in movies because then we have completely separate pictures taken at a rate of 24 per second and projected at the same speed. Let's describe the position of one spoke of a wheel as if it were the hour hand of a clock. Let's suppose the wheel is turning clockwise and at a special speed. Suppose that in 1/24th of a second (the time between pictures) one spoke of the wheel doesn't make a full turn. Suppose that in one picture it is straight up at the 12 o'clock position, and in the next picture it has turned only to the 11 o'clock position. And so on. You can see that even if the wheel is turning forward (clockwise), it will seem to be turning backward.

TV gives the effect for just the same basic reason, although pictures on a TV screen are more complex and they come at a different rate, I believe 30 pictures per second.

Why does cabbage grow above ground and a carrot grow under the ground?

Ann Jacobe
Island Lake, Illinois

Of course, you know that both have parts both places. Almost all garden plants have the same kinds of parts. They have roots and stems and leaves. And most of them make seeds. Some kinds of plants, like lettuce and cabbage, make leaves that are good to eat. Some, like carrots and turnips, make big fleshy roots that are good. And some, like wheat and corn and rice, make seeds that we eat.

Out of all the very many kinds of plants on earth we have picked a few to grow because they have a part that is good to eat. There is no law that says you can't eat a corn root or a carrot leaf if you want to. But these are not likely to be very good food, and I doubt that you will ever find them in supermarkets.

My brother and I found some seashell fossils. We can't explain why there are those type fossils in this area because our area is very hilly. We don't know if the ocean came up to here or not. Can you explain it?

Patrick Walker
Waco, Texas

I think it is not really any great surprise to find seashell fossils near Waco where you live. There are also many of them where I live near Austin.

Of course, it does seem a surprise at first because this part of the country is hilly and a long way from the seacoast. The face of our earth has changed a lot in its long, long history. Finding fossils of marine animals shows you that this part of the earth must have been under the ocean when those animals were alive millions of years ago.

NORTH AMERICA: 75 MILLION YEARS AGO

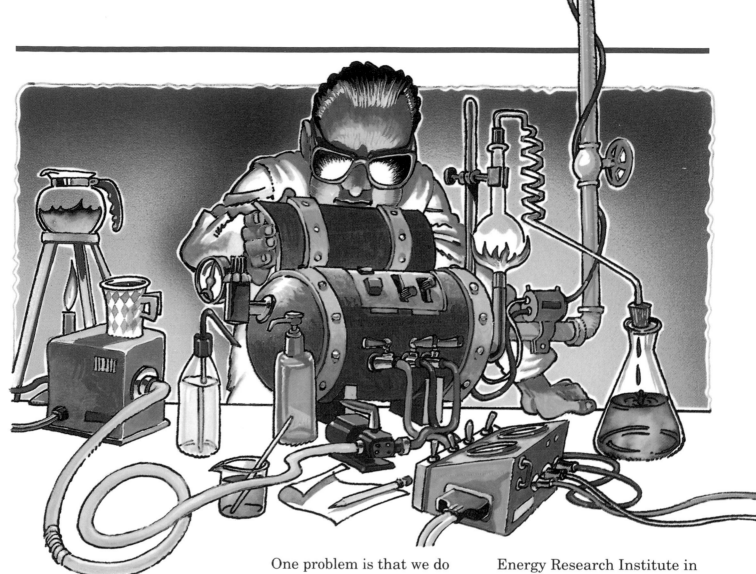

Has anyone ever tried to make oil? If they could figure out how the decaying material was changed into oil, couldn't they just use a similar process but speed it up?

Anna Shoeman
Biddeford, Maine

I think that's a good question and a good idea. It is so good that there must be some reason why we are not doing that right now.

One problem is that we do not know exactly how oil (petroleum) was made. The most common idea is that it was made from the fats and oils of algae (or plankton). There is not any big mass of algae grown anywhere in any one year. But our oil, some of it deep within the ground, could have been made very slowly. It seems to have been made and stored up over more than a hundred million years. We are using up the oil much faster than it could have been made. So that's the second problem: if we made oil from algae growing in nature, we could not make it fast enough.

You might like to know that some scientists at the Solar Energy Research Institute in Golden, Colorado, are working on an idea like yours. They are trying to see if we could grow algae a lot faster than algae grow in nature and maybe find special kinds that makes lots of fats and oils. The idea is to change solar energy into the stored-up energy in vegetable oil. That isn't quite the same as petroleum that we get out of the ground, but it does have lots of energy. There is no doubt that we can do this. The question is how much that kind of oil would cost.

I really don't think your idea would work. But you should not be discouraged. I have had lots of bright ideas that never worked.

53

Why does lightning prefer to hit high places rather than low?

Rheanna Doncses
Valrico, Florida

Lightning occurs as a discharge of electricity. Usually there has been a big accumulation of negative charge at the lower levels of a cloud. The discharge is like a big spark going through the air toward the ground. Air is not very good at conducting electricity. Almost anything that sticks up high makes a better pathway. So, anything that sticks up high is more likely to get hit by lightning.

Lightning will often hit a tall tree. A tall metal building, like the Empire State Building, is still better. Like water running downhill, a negative electric charge seeking a positive charge will take the easiest path.

Some people say that there are no living things on the Moon, but I think that the astronauts put living things on the Moon. Do you think so?

Sylvia Huang
New Rochelle, New York

I think you are right that the astronauts, even though they tried to be very clean, must have left some bacteria on the surface of the Moon. That happened in the early 1970s.

One reason to suppose that there is no life on the Moon is that it's not a very friendly place for life. Temperatures change from way below zero at night to more than 100° Celsius in full sunlight. There isn't any water, and there's no air. So it's likely that any bacteria the astronauts took to the Moon have long since died out.

I think we can safely say that there is probably no life on the Moon.

What are cosmic rays?

Jeff Nichols
Davenport, Iowa

When scientists were first learning about radioactive elements, they invented instruments for detecting the radiation coming off. One of these is called a Geiger counter. It counts, usually with clicks you can hear, ionizations in air produced by X rays and high-speed particles.

When a Geiger counter is brought close to radioactive material, like radium or uranium, it clicks away rapidly and tells about how much radiation is there. But there was a surprise that no matter where they were, Geiger counters always slowly clicked away. They clicked still more slowly with shields of lead around them or when placed in mines deep in the earth. Finally, it turned out that some radiation is coming to us from outer space. That is called cosmic rays.

Study has shown that cosmic rays are high-speed particles, the nuclei of atoms. They seem to come from outside the solar system, maybe from exploding stars.

More cosmic rays are detected at high altitude, so the blanket of our air screens out most of them and not many are left at ground level. Someone has estimated that the energy in cosmic rays is about the same as starlight. I suspect that the astronauts in walking on the Moon received more cosmic rays than you will in your lifetime. So, you should not worry about them. I don't.

What happens to stuff that falls into a black hole?

Patrick Walker
Waco, Texas

I do not know much about black holes except the idea of how they are formed.

At some time in its very long life, a star may use up the nuclear energy that keeps it in the form of a hot gas. Then it contracts and gets smaller. It may become a dwarf star with all its matter squeezed more tightly together. However, if it was very large to start with, it will have a very great mass and pull of gravity. The idea is that maybe the force pulling all that stuff together can get so great that it crushes itself down to almost nothing at all.

A black hole is a place where not even light can escape. That's why it's called a black hole. So I guess that anything that fell in would get crushed down to almost nothing at all.

What is the smallest mammal?

Anna Shih
New Hudson, Michigan

The smallest mammal in the world is a kind of shrew. Shrews look like very small mice, except that they have more sharply pointed noses. Few people ever see a shrew because the creatures are so small and they stay in hiding much of the time. Shrews are also said to be the shortest-lived mammals on earth. Some of them grow up and become mature in about six months, then grow old and die in a year or so.

The smallest shrew lives in parts of Europe and Africa. It has a body length of about $1^{1}/_{2}$ inches, and a tail of about an inch. It is called the white-toothed pigmy shrew. The smallest mammal in the United States is also a shrew. It is also called a pigmy shrew, but it is perhaps a wee bit larger than the ones that live in Europe and Africa. Our pigmy shrew lives in parts of Canada and in the eastern part of the United States. It weighs two or three grams, which is about the same weight as a dime!

Shrews have one of the biggest appetites of any mammal. They hunt food most of the time they are awake, and they eat many times a day. One kind can eat its own weight in a single meal, and two or three times its weight in a day and a night. I doubt if a pig could eat this much. Maybe we should say that people who eat too much eat like a shrew, instead of like a pig.

O.P.B.

I have a question for you. We live by a lake. My sister, Melissa, and I have been skating on it several times. We have heard strange noises coming from the lake when it is frozen. It happened right under me once! We can also hear them from our house. They are very loud. Can you tell me what they are?

Michelle Wang
Germantown, Maryland

If the noises you hear are like sharp cracks with some rumblings, I think they are made by the ice. As you know, ice expands as it freezes. That's what makes it float. That also tends to squeeze the ice outward. As ice freezes and thaws and freezes again, it does all sorts of pushing and shoving that makes it crack and rumble. You can play that it is talking to you.

Why is the sky blue, and what makes it?

Melissa Martin
Satsuma, Alabama

The sky is blue because of the small scattering of sunlight by molecules of gases in the air, mostly by nitrogen molecules. We think of air as being clear and transparent—and it is. We think of sunlight as being almost white—and it is.

But in going thousands of miles through our atmosphere, a tiny amount of sunlight is scattered. When that happens, blue light rays are scattered more than red light rays—in fact, about six times more. So, the light that is scattered down to us from the sky looks blue. I'm glad that happens. If it did not, the sky would look black.

Index